DINOSAUR HOUR

poems by

Biman Roy

Finishing Line Press
Georgetown, Kentucky

DINOSAUR HOUR

Copyright © 2020 by Biman Roy
ISBN 978-1-64662-352-5 First Edition
All rights reserved under International and Pan-American Copyright Conventions. No part of this book may be reproduced in any manner whatsoever without written permission from the publisher, except in the case of brief quotations embodied in critical articles and reviews.

ACKNOWLEDGMENTS

Grateful acknowledgement is made to the editors of the following publications where poems or versions of these poems first appeared:

Before The Meticulous Scalpel ~ *The Full Circle Journal*, 2003 (On Line)
Painting Lesson ~ *Hampden-Sydney Poetry Review*, 2007
Chairs on the Lawn ~ *Hubbub*, Spring 2007
Wall Street; Miscarriage ~ *The Louisville Review*, Fall 2006
Naming Of Flowers ~ *Porcupine*, Fall 2006
Door ~ *Phantasmagoria*, Fall 2007
Wordsmith; Fame ~ *RiverSedge*, Spring 2007
August Manifesto ~ *Nimrod International*, Spring 2008
Red Carpet ~ *Meridian Anthology of Poetry*, Summer 2008
Dinosaur Hour ~ *Quiddity International*, Fall 2009
Anthropocene ~ *Controlled Burn*, Spring 2010
Cat; Jacaran; Shadow; Picnic Ravished ~ *The Poetic Bond* VIII 2018

Publisher: Leah Huete de Maines
Editor: Christen Kincaid
Cover Art: *The journey* by Glenn Losack, MD
Author Photo: Glenn Losack, MD
Cover Design: Elizabeth Maines McCleavy

Order online: www.finishinglinepress.com
also available on amazon.com

Author inquiries and mail orders:
Finishing Line Press
P. O. Box 1626
Georgetown, Kentucky 40324
U. S. A.

Table of Contents

Anthropocene 1

Naming of Flowers 2

The Amphibian Hour 3

Before the Meticulous Scalpel 4

Wall Street 5

Picnic, Ravished 6

Fame 7

Painting Lesson 8

Playtime 9

Door 10

Cat, Jacaranda, Shadow 11

Eclipse 12

Dinosaur Hour 13

Miscarriage 14

Middle-Aged, Promontory, Nothingness 16

Midway 17

The Man Does Not Have To 18

Red Carpet 19

Walking Past the Porch 20

August Manifesto 21

Wordsmith 22

Chairs on the Lawn 23

Meteor 24

For Amitabha Chaudhury
(1946–2020)

In poetry and friendship

ANTHROPOCENE

These flocculent jasmine
on rectangles of burnt sienna
declare the first snow

as a girl grows
into the burden of her breasts,
a slow affluence,

and I know it's only October.

The laced curtain of light
still caresses the Halloweened
hedge of my neighbor's yard,

sky, dimmed and dumbfounded,
struggles to maintain sanity,

but I get distracted
by this white opulence
that puts its feet flat on my face and asks

"Are you ready to unmoor?"

NAMING OF FLOWERS

"And today we have naming of parts..."
—Henry Reed

Linnaeus treated flowers with respect
but pontificated on their sex lives
upsetting the Bishop of Carlisle.

With a flair he named them
after his esteemed colleagues,
Gardenia, Camellia, Rudbeckia,
and preferred the company
of pollinated pistils.

Roses have a knack for being
mistresses of distinguished men
as tulips do for dukes and princes;
each has its own ax to grind
 like a rose hiding the crooked tooth
of Empress Josephine.

When gods and goddesses make love,
crocuses burst forth from their ardor.
 Flowers like lady's mantle, are down to earth
bringing *lust to the worke of generacyon.*

Some prefer to lead. Iris guides
the desolate souls
on an iridescent bridge, while flowering
quinces take an impassable stance
 against the deepening winter.

They all stagger in a playful passion.

While looking at her stepson,
Phaedra pricked the leaves
and the lover of Lady Chatterley
adorns the Lady's maiden hair
with forget-me-nots.

THE AMPHIBIAN HOUR

Out of their longing for a session at Sorbonne,
three Bostonians dined on canned sardines
and red ale at the amphibian hour.

Boys wearing denim and a Santayana smile
outmaneuvered adults
while women flaunted their breast implants
like Olympic gold.

Afterward,
a rustle in gabardines, serge, and tweeds.

Somewhere a green bulb rising into pink petals,
gold and orange of maples settling on
cold gunmetal of the bay.
so much New England-like—

Not too far from here
a mausoleum
waits
to encase immortality.

BEFORE THE METICULOUS SCALPEL

Imagine Leonardo
and his first autopsy lesson,
or the boy looking at the innards
of the first computer
through its glass enclosure!

Before the meticulous scalpel
a door unhinges.

The body is its own metaphor.
It holds organs
like a jewelry box, sworn to secrecy.

Vital juices,
viridian, vermillion, pearly white
unperturbed in caverns,
awaiting signals of a storm
while ziggurats of muscle
secured to promontories
anticipate a tremble.

Imagine light
sequestered in translucent vats,
oval, scaphoid, and cuneiform,
an anarchy of passion
waiting to reign,
then a sudden swarm of musical bones,
ulna, fibula, calcaneus, manubrium.

As the sand settles
in the hour-glass of night,
inquisitive heads tilt back
to get a glimpse. The heart-lamp
shines through the skin.

WALL STREET

Wind painted high
almost to the ceiling,
the room is luminously
silent as closed vowel,
barges arrive and depart
from the edge of her lap.

"What is she reading?"

Standing far away as she reads
I feel the fall quicken
loosening its music
on stark streets.

Out there Wall Street is closing
Times in hand a man waiting
under the bridge
in a muffled stink
of unopened garbage

for a taxi or death.

PICNIC, RAVISHED

Last night there was too much commotion
over small things.
  "Falling in love or falling apart—
what difference does it make? "I said

 "What hinges
        between words is more lethal,"
my lover added.

          After this wintry slumber,

                fireworks of forsythia
                     add luster
                   to half-shut eyes.

       We sat cross-legged on wet green carpet
       and ravished our boxed lunch,
       banter banishing any heaviness in the air.

          Smoking on a bench, guarded by leafy branches, I thought,

          even in this rancor the peach tree
          pines for the lone bear
          to tear up the flesh and suck its pulp.

FAME

Every age has its invisible boundaries
            beyond which there is isolation
and death.

Each lover knows the edge
where love turns bloody.

It was Leonardo's insatiable hunger for knowledge
that made him unpopular;

when he painted primrose women
and rubicund men,
        people rejoiced,
and rejoiced again for his confounding contraptions.

But when he poked scalpels
into dead men's flesh
to draw his vessels and ligaments

or waited for the old to die
        to dig their bones,
parishioners screamed necromancy.

While dying in the royal palace
he drew up his will
for the young lover/apprentice
and whispered,
"Let all my fame be yours, Oh my lover king."

PAINTING LESSON

You must not take light lightly.

    Watch Delacroix's spendthriftness
    or Monet's delight.

You must go to the source:

    a lamp, the sun
    or the breath of moon through a chiffon curtain.

Sprinkle a few photons

    to draw the halo out of each object

    when you are in
    a tight corner and shadows menace;

    Only then, the skin glows,
    the pitcher shows its fullness,
    and the brass plate rim bruises
    the peachiness
        of the pile of peaches.

PLAYTIME

The piano player
        is by now with his aproned wife,
   drinking soup with his head bent
              as if in a prayer.

The sky looks grim
with bales of singed cotton
piling on its gray courtyard.

Tall trees look taller and ominous,
birds dig their claws into bark.

For some
        this is the playtime.
This is when musicians
pick up their saxophones, quiet as
cleaned and gagged shotguns.
They play as if for the last time,
a few bars of sound
squeezed through faded
              columns of light.

Now the piano player
is back at his piano to slice
the silence with the sword of Bach.

DOOR

Neither the wind nor words,
        not a persistent pressing shoulder
of an arm tied to groceries
or a debt of neighbor's blood,

   like a small unnamable wish
or the intent in the bird's brain
just before flight,

opened the door, by itself
        it opened for someone or no one.

Unbothered by past sense
the door opened a little
and stayed open.

It caused no harm or ruckus,
        let breaths and shadows pass
with equal justice
and an allotment of space,

like air parting thin lips of leaves,
unholding their chatter.

CAT, JACARANDA, SHADOW

The czar who ordered the slaughter of innocents
and tortured his own blood,
also wept with music.

His tears made the arbor weep.

This soft lay of cat in the sun,
the lone jacaranda with its promise of flowers,
and the not-so-distant lake in a quilt of aching mist—

will I take these with me if I were to die today?

Henry the hare is yet to come to my lawn.
He will dip his paws in grass and meditate
as the sky will turn viridian in his orange eyes.

Speaking of the sky and its vast, blue dome
reminds me of the Roman Empire and its pride.

Does penitence help prepare one better for death?

This is my armor if I were to die today.
This indefinite lay of cat,
this prolific jacaranda
        and Henry's shadow

on the pulpit of my lawn, and the memory
of the Roman Empire—
a slow sweep of silt in an emerald lake.

ECLIPSE

The evening was a mess
                and enmeshed in it
were echoes of falling dishes.

"I told you so from the beginning."
"Shall we be formal or let-go-ish?"
She hissed through her teeth, unbared.

The sneer jabbed at the place
that could tickle and hurt
                at the same time.

What else could one do? I thought,
in this voluptuous weather
when it rained Malt and Malbec
except to shut the door and wait.

Dogs sniffed the air and curled up.
Then a tremble in the wind—
as if someone had
slit the throat of the moon.

DINOSAUR HOUR

Deep in the orchard,
    velvety peaches
    with teeth mark around nipples
    get ripe with desire.

    The road winds up in the cloud.

From cracked skull of earth
a century of prayers fly
like a jet of bats skyward.

    There is a time for small creatures,
    then there is the dinosaur hour.

    A thistle, a thicket,
    a cloud, a cloister,
    a time for all happy moments
    accounted for
    and indented.

MISCARRIAGE

Body arches backwards as you turn
against light casting an enormous
shadow almost touching the edge
of evening.
        What mouth owns,
mind strives to transcend.

Sterile forceps, scissors, and sutures,
the cleaned bones of winter
glint and stare as rarefied ribs
stripped of their pride.

Last year we were in Arkansas
playing in flat-chested fields,
wheat-rippled.
Young plants, supple as lily stalks,
brushed against our inner thighs,
gave us ambition.

We waited
for the first rumble and you pressed
my hands tightly,

the way you press now, only tighter.

Plump fingers of the technician
hold a cold knob close to the skin
between umbilicus and mons pubis.
Her auburn hair catching fire,
the dying light slanted on blood-soaked gauze
and gondolas of gold moored under maple.

Don't know where we will be this winter.
Maybe in New Hampshire,
in secluded cold quarters,
still aching for Florida,
with you reading Freud's letters
and me, brooding over flawed menstruation

and an occasional egret
like a slow syllable of snow unfurling
in the empty womb of these wintry depths.

MIDDLE-AGED, PROMONTORY, NOTHINGNESS
"Maturity, a stationary sense—as, I suppose…"
—Philip Larkin

It is too much to wish for.
The sad candelabra, the epithet on the wall, a fixed smile,
dead centuries pressed tight as bookmarks,
even the mole on the medial aspect of the left breast,
once dreamt about, are like chameleons of invariant colors
genetically downgraded to ordinary lizards.

All roads don't lead to Bethlehem.
Circling around like an eagle of boredom,
One cruises back to the same bald acacia.

The silence now purse-strings us.
The music eludes and reiterates
the moments at lakefront nights.
No one knows what presages the doldrums,
Only an assumption of uncertainty weaves the air
like the smoke of a first barbecue.

A pair of fur-lined gloves on snow,
leftover wine, whiffs of perfume,
funny stories, half-told,
kept frozen in the hourglass.

The body begs to be forgiven.
It's all broken into and damaged,
like the eyes of birds that have lost their nests and eggs
in a storm and burn with blue fury.

As often happens,
this will all slowly crumble
into a pile of dumb rocks,
meaningless and enormously empty,
no difference between the road taken and not taken.

MIDWAY

Don't know which way the lever turns.

Toward left, an amorphous heap of reassurance
or toward right, a whirling storm of rejection.

Back in the upstate
I built a whole lot of contraptions
with steel rivets, girdles, and pulleys
to make a part of life disappear.

But it always returns at odd hours of the day
like a banished alley cat, memory- licked.

I fought for a life that was hushed as a tombstone
and felt like an inmate in a twelve by eight cell,
scared to be bludgeoned to death.

But something happened in the midway,
when the moon rose above the blue bonnet
of the Alleghany Mountain
to expose perfect ankles, passion-scalded.

THE MAN DOES NOT HAVE TO

The man does not have to come back to this house
which sits still among pines, cold as a doorknob,
with tiny windows and a damp floor.

He may decide otherwise,
may be precise or conciliatory,
barge in or enter with a bow.
Anytime is auspicious
which he chooses or does not choose.

The wicker rocker, the red mat with Indian motif,
the pitcher with Cleopatra's headgear,
the lacquered desk and, above all,
the oversized, rustic bed—
will wait for him to share his warmth,
a rare commodity when the wood stove is unlit.

If he chooses not to,
someone else might fill it.

As he chooses not to come back
to this house or to any house,
he will walk through uncut grass and unwieldy branches,
sand between his toes, and an occasional moon
until the sea bites into the sky.

Once in the sea,
he will decide whether to swim or sail

or disappear

RED CARPET

And suddenly this fiery orchestra—
along the palisades,
spouts spilling rumors

        on maple to oak to fir:

light jumps like a spring
out of a mechanical songbird.

Its urgency propels the shaft of air
to the dock where sleepy ships
emerge from a rambling night.
They queue up with coffee mugs.

Pigeons take flight
over dumpsters, barracks, acropolis,
and acres of fallow lots
cradling bent bodies of Toyota and Dodge.

Then a slow settle,
slower than blood,
much slower than mercy

and everything is once again
back to its orbit:
child's toy, mangy dog, computers—

Oh the old king's blood-red carpet
waits to be unrolled and blessed
across the sky.

WALKING PAST THE PORCH

The sky is an illusion,
unspecial, its orange
turns mauve,
turns slate, turns black.

The sky holds no promise,
a regular job well done
in a full-bodied spirit.

The willow contemplates
the oncoming loneliness of winter
at the miller's pond, shivers a little.

Children are back from the ball field.
The house rattles like all houses
along the train track,
passage of an outbound train,
a sign of respect like trees to the wind.

The dog starts to bark
then decides not. Crickets on the lawn
are as silent as birds, stalled in their circle.

A man walks past the porch
or a shadow of a man
or recollection of a man
walking past yesterday
or a few summer evenings ago,

head bent, lost in thought
like Matisse walking in a park in Paris
thinking of space or arrangements in space
as if to map out our solitude,

or fence it in.

AUGUST MANIFESTO

What comes back
can also amble away,
rose-scent
bordering on winter.

      Turning toward the door
means emptiness.

Hands, still and dozing
on the quilt of your belly
like a pair of iguana on the windowsill.

      All questions are either
stifled or answered away.

I lie naked in the same room
year after year.

      What evanesce in lowlight
has the possibility
to tiptoe back.

Eyes held unblinking
may be for this
or for nothing.

 Will the tongue-tied moon
stop circling the oak someday?

WORDSMITH

Working men
      love to be in masks,
whether a blow torch
      or a syringe.
Even war is work,
stacking bones,
cleaning daggers.

What do poets do?
      "My hands are useless,"
Neruda laments.

Once the goods are
wheeled, unloaded,
and shutters drawn,
the poets take accounts
of all herons, viceroys,
oaks, and deer,
burning midnight blood.

CHAIRS ON THE LAWN

One chair for rumor,
        one for consolation,
and another for atonement.

        Beyond that, a cocoon of sleep
hangs loosely, letting its milk-light
spill into night.

you don't even ask questions.
        Inviting hands are brushed away
like sudden spiderwebs
en route to the garden.

Laziness of summer afternoons—

what is left over of a day's worth
can be canned as phrases from Li Po.

No clipper in the spice route,
no stag in the clearing,
guests all gone, also the ancestors.

What if you rearrange the chairs—

will it be different?

Say, one for remorse,
one for reconciliation,
one for ardor
or even happiness.

And what if you forget
or decide not to?

METEOR

Walking in the woods
as a monologue,
no familiar tree to lean on,
no eager fight to pick,
no discreet pain to fight with,
only a vague recollection
like images in old movies
from an imagined childhood
fleeting across the snowscape.

Mind, bare as winter.

What can I do
with this substantial space
at this limitless hour?

It is what the dead
are destined to go through
before they are salvaged.

Then they regain their memories;
the aspen,
the wren,
the phlox,
even the moon,
one by one,
as they ascend the ladder.

Biman Roy has been writing and publishing his poetry for more than 30 years in various literary magazines in the United States, United Kingdom, Canada, and India. Some of which include: *Nimrod, The Alembic, The Briar Cliff Review, Controlled Burn, Still* (UK), *Hampden-Sydney Poetry Review, Harper Palate, Hubbub, Louisville Review, Meridian Anthology of Contemporary Poetry, Mobius: The Poetry Magazine, Quiddity, The Owen Wister Review, Permafrost, Phantasmagoria, Porcupine, RiverSedge, ARIEL: A Review of International English Literature* (Canada), *Schuylkill Valley Journal, The South Carolina Review, Westview, Youth Times* (India), and *Xavier Review.*

Biman's writing has been nominated for Best of the Net and the Pushcart award and his chapbook of prose poems, *Of Moon and Washing Machine* has recently been published by Uncollected Press. Some of his writing interests encompass poetry, plays, fiction and mental health related journal articles. He is passionate about the art of moviemaking, Eastern music as well as American Jazz music and paints when time permits.

As a psychiatrist, Biman serves as a consultant for hospitals in the greater New York area.

He is also a Distinguished Life Fellow of the American Psychiatric Association and lives in Ridgewood, New Jersey.

www.ingramcontent.com/pod-product-compliance
Lightning Source LLC
LaVergne TN
LVHW041519070426
835507LV00012B/1676